Book One of the Laugh & Learn with Lily Series

Why Do I Have A Tummy Ache?

Alyana Veras

Illustrations By:
Alexis Calderon

1.888.5069.NOW
www.nowscpress.com
@nowscpress

Ordering Information:
Quantity sales. Special discounts are available on quantity purchases by corporations, associations, and others. For details, contact the publisher at the address above. Orders by U.S. trade bookstores and wholesalers. Please contact: NOW SC Press: Tel: (888) 5069-NOW or visit www.nowscpress.com.

Printed in the United States of America

First Printing, 2017

ISBN: 978-0-9995845-3-8

NOW
SC PRESS

Dedication

I want to dedicate this book to Arielys and Azeylia, who inspire me to write books not only for them, but for young minds all over the world.

Lily was a little girl with
a big love for **sweets**.

In fact, they were the only things
she'd ever want to eat.

One day,
while her mommy was mopping the basement floor,

Lily snuck into the kitchen and opened the pantry door.

She found a secret box filled with goodies
oh-so-yummy

and couldn't help but wonder
what they'd feel like
in her tummy.

She reached for a **cookie**
and waved it in the air

and started singing softly
of the **snacks**
that waited there.

"Candy, candy sugar sweet,
a marshmallow and graham cracker treat.

Lollipops and doughnut holes,
ice cream in a waffle cone bowl."

"Candy, candy wrapped in smiles,
milk chocolate in giant piles.
Gumdrops dressed in rainbow colors,
cupcakes baked with eggs and butter."

She took one bite and then another,
as she was hiding from her mother.

She ate
and ate
and ate some more

of sweets
and candies
and cakes galore.

After she **chewed** and **slurped**
and **munched**

and **licked**
and **gobbled**
and **tasted**
and
crunched,

she went to settle down for bed
and rest her sleepy little head.

Uh oh!   Her tummy
was starting
to hurt.

It was rumbling under her
candy-stained shirt.

Her **tooth** was **achy** and her **head** was too.
Poor Lily didn't know what to do.

Her mom walked in and shook her head.
"Too much dessert can hurt,"
she said.

"Fill your stomach with
healthy things

like watermelons
and string beans."

"Your body will thank you by growing **tall** and your tummy won't hurt, **not at all.**

So instead of sucking on **lollipops,** eat some yogurt with berries on top."

"Okay," Lily said. "I'll try really hard to stop eating too many chocolates and tarts.

"A healthy snack is all I need.

May I have an **apple**, please?"

Did you love the story? Look for Book Two in the Laugh & Learn with Lily Series, available in 2018: *Will You Teach Me How to Swim?*

Lily wants to learn how to swim, but she's scared of the water. In her newest adventure, she learns how to conquer her fear and start swimming!

About the Author

Alyana is a stay-at-home mom to two girls. She has a special love for writing and seeks to inspire and educate young minds through her books. She attributes her talent to the Lord, and continually receives motivation and support from her husband.

She is excited and ready to continue writing children's books for many years to come.

NOW
SC PRESS

www.ingramcontent.com/pod-product-compliance
Lightning Source LLC
Chambersburg PA
CBHW042020090426
42811CB00015B/1695